T0063997

A Fairy's Story

A Fairy's Story

Poems of love and philosophy

Manali Bonde

PARTRIDGE

A Penguin Random House Company

To order additional copies of this book, contact
Partridge India
000 800 10062 62
orders.india@partridgepublishing.com

www.partridgepublishing.com/india

Contents

Words before poems...1
Image 1: Leaf of Love 2
Part I: Love 3
1.   A fairy's story...5
2.   Invasion...7
3.   Marvel 8
4.   Sometime later may be 9
5.   Mother & her child...11
6.   Without you 13
7.   Man who kissed blue girl.......................................14
8.   Orange hue 19
9.   Painted words..20
10. Love you 21
11. Just a fluke 23
12. Stroll away..24
13. Name I hear..25
14. Dilemma 27
15. Dog's query...29
16. Don't walk away...30
17. Sometimes..31
18. Yearning..33
19. Blame...34
20. Park..35
21. Everyday 36
22. Passing me..37
23. You...38
24. Dance in the rain...39
25. Beautiful evening 40

Image 2: Thoughts from Ellora 42
Part II: Philosophy & Love 43
1.   Sympathy.. 45
2.   A girl described... 46
3.   Delusional dream.. 49
4.   How to survive... 50
5.   A rose in my yard.. 52
6.   White paper gifts 53
7.   A sad storm 55
8.   Decisions 57
9.   Or... 58
10. Game of love.. 59
11. Weirdness 60
12. I ask myself.. 61
13. What I want? 63
14. Sailing of my life.. 64
15. Blank page 65
16. Agony or guilt 66
17. Silly emotions 67
18. Shiny bond... 68
19. Zeal... 70
20. Question 71
21. Prologue 73
22. Sounds 74
23. Invitation 75
24. Rain... 77
25. Distance 78

Image 3: Rays of sun on glass and thorns......................80
Part III: Philosophy..81
1.   Tell me your fear..83
2.   Attention 86
3.   Picture 87
4.   Awaken..88
5.   Secret desire 89
6.   Bridge of the waterfall 90
7.   Wait 93
8.   World to a loser..94
9.   Insecurity..96
10.   Alive Mirror...98
11.   Existence...99
12.   Hail the leader..100
13.   A day...101
14.   An outsider jaw...102
15.   Song & the storyteller 103
16.   The grief..105
17.   The light & its wisdom................................106
18.   Raindrops...108
19.   Fighting souls 109
20.   Traveller..111
21.   Proud heart 113
22.   Self protection...114
23.   Words of black ink......................................115
24.   Light and shadows......................................116
25.   Entrapment...117

*To all those who dare to be weird
and ask for happiness in life*

Words before poems

Poems are an easy way to experience a particular moment. We have many happy, sad moments in our life. Sometimes we want to remember them always and sometimes we just throw them away as nightmare. These moments of different emotions leave clue to life's philosophy. Philosophy is not complicated word if we try to understand our self step by step.

'Darshan shastra' is the philosophy stated in Vedas and Upanishads. Poems of fairy's story are inspired mostly from this philosophy. Dharshan shastra had many different sub schools of philosophy. Schools were based on the factor they gave most importance. Some gave to the way of the traveller, some to the object and some to the work.

In all everything is related, we need to join the pieces from here to there. Many concepts of philosophy help psychology, further if we try they can be related to physics in some aspects. These poems try to relate the two different factors.

Thus, to enjoy these poems at most, it can be advised to read them by keeping aside every thought and ideas which are previously known. Finally I hope to find this book inspiration for new thoughts and Ideas for self discovery.

Part I: Love

1.   A fairy's story

He seeks the fairy of his dreams
A simple thing a prince to care love
But is it she the fairy with wings?
Or does he needs the wing to love
A question to term fairy of dreams

Questions are raised when he goes
Day may be each to just see again
And Fairy to sit beside him attained
She sympathises the child her lover
But credence lays side which more?

Power has the fairy to prince' ruin
But use what of with austere mind
Deluded mind empowers him of all
To think he can love and she too him
Infatuates power him the love idea

Around the waist desires he hand
And true it is that hers is curve belle
She questions though whose hand
An impressionist or inquirer it is?
Perplexity fairy likes indulgence in

Because she loves a heretic of time,
So can never devote to great divine
Has he a thick brow and grey eyes
And manner of no pity but serenity
Fairy finds his psalms enchanting

The condition which forsakes happy
Is he to find not around her but where
Pursues the heretic her not than art
Dilemma then of want & need creeps
Phase she describes it to be passed on

And passes when she strong willed
Wings now could fly her to freedom
Separation sought her sombre beauty
Reclined she bonds of prince waiting
Long before it was, ascetic now arrives

Moon when one arrives, stars too
Telling that of nester's aspire to kiss
For her ascetic solitude he to break
Fairy but thwarts ardent advent lips
Bids, to hold her tears in empty palm

And he does close them in earnest
Then could she see the love in rays
Credence was of the faith undefined
Magus he is to tweak time, defining
Fairy's and own soul to coral shrine

2. Invasion

Within the veil of my heart
There are things intimate
Should it be known really?
A secret couldn't easily be disclosed
Terrified to be discovered by you
With only desire to be also
To be searched by you, abrupt
When you do, it is an invasion
When you don't, a child angers
The solution you need to find
As the way you see me forever
With the eyes of sparkling love
Reply I with the hasty glances
Fragrance of my melting heart
Just for you to know, I too!

3. Marvel

There I see a graceful girl
Leaning on the sole tree
Taking it to be 'his' arm
Where he could be?

I see him, sitting restlessly
On bench, just so near the tree
Much so, wanting her beside him
Why is she like that every time?

Seeing them like this there
Wonders nature the complexity
Of the simple word "love"
What's the matter between them?

Could it just be that? And it is!
Both wake up from there trance
To say a little bit to each other
Isn't it getting a bit confusing?

I see them suddenly stop
A silence of gazing each other
And finally a gleeful hug
What more marvellous should be!

4. Sometime later may be

Some time later may be...
We won't have anything to share
We won't have anything to talk
Such an irony, is it a love or separation?

Some time later may be...
There won't be a question,
Of trust between us
Neither or either of us will do each other

Some time later maybe...
People will stand for us
For their contribution in ceremony
Of bringing together or separating, of our worlds

Some time later maybe...
I would still love you as ever
May be you would also
But the relation ours- would be unnamed

Some time later may be...
It will be grand merriment to see you
And awful pain, at the same
In minds-"thinking you of me the same?"

Some time later may be...
We won't be desperate
We won't be immature
Only the craving remains for each other

Some time later may be...
There will be new moon and new sun
And new us, but together
To start again newly different or as same

5.   Mother & her child

There is a second
When I think of mother
As someone deeply I know
Coming with me from ever

She is the reason
Of never ending love in me
She is the reason
For the hate of hatred around

I see the extra patience
When I forget to apologize
For the trifle-grave mistakes
Remorsefully realized later

Sometimes world is blank
Mother fills the emptiness
Reminding me always
No one can take her place

So much known is to her
Even something of me
Unknown to me and my heart
Just as her inbuilt person

I pray to god as a lover
Of my mother's smile
To last it forever
As happiness her eternity

What a tough...
Yet a happy job!
To understand a mother
Without a single sob

A bond beautiful forms
Between a mother and child
And the child later also
Of her own child

6.   Without you

Callous is the rain
To hit the earth below
Petals of your eyes...
I see, they slowly rise

Nature...isn't that a miracle!
That we admire between us
They hope for your best
I wish you eternity of best

Wake me...wake me up
You wouldn't want to know
The quiet dream I have
You read easily within me

Don't have a bold heart
To lose you from my life
But courage to suffer
Living without you a life

Rebel and rebellious
Is my mind, at most,
When I see you around
To be sober in front of you

Should I quit?
Should I start?
To pray for me,
To justify you of my memories

7.   Man who kissed blue girl

Unaware is the crowd of just
Suppose they should to result
There lives a guy noble at eye
Looks at me with weirdest call
Could I say more but inferior
Feeling comes to mind always
Brows his dark and to the point
Makes me want to touch them
End to end dragging my finger
Not it began though such as it

The culprit thick of my thoughts
Are the thoughts of sensitive
Sickening me for very myself
Painted I am blue such as blue
My life ever have been of birth
But the thickness were created
Of protection and pity by around
Who love, few they have been!
A work of meagre nobody had
Existence mine to gain meaning

Shined warm rays orange a sun
Making him come in the air
Calculating the accounts of bare
Didn't I see when it happened?
The attention drone to me his
Shy I am not, tears been shed
To make strong culprit within
But the thought to talk is more
Forbidding finding happiness
Not really destined already is

But the finery described be not
His, how could I resist to do so!
Strong is his image to be out
My wit holds on even in absence
Blue is his blood as royal a valor
And rides the blackest of horse
Looks at me with glance curious
And talks as if first time in life
Opened his mouth to address
Questions of child to a mother

Wonder what purpose of him
King has in his court so civil
Though he is younger in years
Then king or kingdom and me
Followed are his eyes in order
To complete the work of civic
But he finds the time better
Always than me so to pursue
Walk may be and to talk me
Every day it is like rule freed

Then a night it is home I walk
Comes as natural he with me
Stammers when simple asked
Seizes wrist in a sudden motion
Says words hazily," I want you,
The rush of eyes, voice kind
All that is you have for yours
Mad is what frantically made
Me, for wanting you in arms
To make it ever worse or fine

Couldn't I think long when seen
Winery in when you beat grapes
To stain blue feet in red shade
Then I would grab hold of them
Right there to drink wine sweet
Call me freak, but I am in love
Married be you wish, I would
Or not you think you'll have me
As a partner, you'll be let free
But let you be mine once for me"

I shout him of fool' arrogance
Talking so directly as infatuate
Raise my voice over him to hide
Craving had been same of mine
So near him makes want more
But reclined be he for the dare
Being not loser he walks away
Angry my heart calls him again
To say things I could never tell
But mouth abstains the melt

Only the utter is "The painting"
Of me, asked him, famous he is
As known in court, also such as
He grins with air resolute, Says
"With the skin blue only but
No colours on it of the clothes"
Resisted I but dare the thought
My mind drags blush to cheeks
Scarf hides it carefully to walk
Leaving him with," we shall see!"

Day and second alike he pursues
To be with me and paint the scene
Agreed on morning at an attic so
With brush and paint he looks
Me with boy' spirit to get prize
Nervous I try to escape in vain
But detaching the final ropes now
Enter I in his eye nearing canvas
To expect a look of rupture or awe
Behold I pain and agony rising

A moment of despair grieves me
To find myself not enough of it
But later to understand reason
Nerves his ache dearly to have
Me not, posed openly to his side
He mourns not showing but mum
But paints he excites on canvas
Violently, me as desire can ever be
Test it is not though I chase pride
Thrashing him more, not giving in

Not pity, craving but overpowers
Days after a moment I walk to him
With a hand slight to touch his face
And kiss with lips readied years ago
Returned with gratitude & solace
Then reader, story here should end
In suspense be our ships of red love
For blue my nature and skin permits
Others be known of a blue blood:
A man who kissed a blue girl

8. Orange hue

Evening with orange hue
A time of soaked feelings
Houses of variety shine
To grayness of my eyes
A cup of brown coffee
With your hands around me
& emotions fast to tell love
Eyes to eyes, to & fro, slowly
It's just a simple kiss
A touch of silent lip to lip
Each other eternity to eternity
There are the colored zeros
To form bond of time
Yet they do not remind end
Just like made for each other
Never arranged or disarranged

9.   Painted words

Behind the painted words
Lies sweet love, yours
Or manifest is it just?
Of acting you as me

Several meanings given
Are by my master mind
Dumb but to sum up
Feelings flow through words

Shiver & intimate feeling
They just refer to you
When I gaze your feel
You steal my entire life

Break me or cut me
Uncontrollable more it is
To be not zipped extremely
Soul to, which is yours

Passion dies, love not
Uprising both vigorously
For the one man only
Forsaken existence in this

10. Love you

Love you still immensely
Can't ask you so much so
As to remember me
Not always but for existence

Love you very deeply
Cutting your presence
Is impossible in heart so
It's just all yours

"Love you!" says I
This I doesn't exist more
It never happened to be mine
I want to say it as separate

Love you forever
I still can't define it
Forever never seems
Coming for even once

'Love you', saying now
So much it hurts
In deep somewhere
To you and only me

Love you my humble,
My dearest weakness
We can't stay together
Nor apart we can be

Love you is the word
I'll keep saying, you only
Till my eyes shut, tight
Not again to see this world

11. Just a fluke

Fluke or by a chance
I found myself one day
Thinking of you, smilingly
Suddenly aware of the change

Fluke or by a chance
I realized joyfully of
Living isn't possible,
Anymore, without you

Fluke or by a chance
How we came across!
Just to mean a little more
Than we ought for each other

Fluke or by a chance
Everything is transformed
So much to be as ever
The world seems wonderful

Fluke or by a chance
I fell in love with you
To just see the happiness
Begin everywhere around

12.   Stroll away

If you could stroll away with me
I would never say no to any slight
Whether it's wild or sane delight
Whatever imagined ever on earth

If you could stroll away with me
Just simply as everything been
On our every earthly day spent
My kiss would rest on your chin

Sun shines no glee to flowers more
Than if you could be away with me
Everything reasons to be perfect
Laws to be broken or be same

But could you joy away with me?
Abandoning the laws of past
Confronting my guilty future then
Running from the mistakes made

Reverse away, instead from me
Not catch nor see you, can so I
It's by flash situation transpired
Let another destroy our affiliation

13. Name I hear

Your face makes me feel
The sudden gush of pinch
My mind decided to take myself
A not usual of self mine it is

Do not you disappear now!
It is the time first I write you
When I stop, nothing remains
To think anything mindlessly else

It is far away when I see
The anything to happen of us
The two points of this 'far'
Are in question on togetherness

Once we met in a long life
Not to start this woeful poem
But something just not the same
As the trees with green leaves

Imagined has my heart in vain
Every way for your substitution
Understanding no dwelling
Yours gave me to reign

It is not hard to live forever
You anywhere near without
Wistful passion rules me
To write words of hatred such

Aloud I call your name once
To want to make you hear
Last time in my voice I say
More than I is in me for you

14.   Dilemma

Logged with brilliance are the days
Sun shines of curious enquiry when
Are the flies seemed to be flying just?
See only them, I the color waves

There you are again and again
Persistent in your appearance
Colors & fades that living me
To feel around my cluttered sanity

I say, there can be too much
Of the between ness of time
Known are all the results when
Patience to be killed every time

Can the proposed way be juggled,
Through the barricades not to be seen
Yours which you satisfy in truly
To extort my being off attention

And there are the pilgrimages we take
Together to make the grass differ
Just might the stupid fate it is
Concealment of nothing it provides

Particularly motioned isn't the way
My poem seeks rebellious streaks
And dare it see that persistence again
There isn't a reason it should be behind

A normal day began that reason
For which I seek the paper now
Necessary are the stupid conversations
To begin the existence of feeling

I wonder day by day and day
For your inquest in me always how
Refusing to show any single drop
Affection which is, further to say

Coax, I try a way to make you mine
Return you the most obstinate corner
Proving none of me on your ever mind
Silence to create it is of unloved loser

Try to forget you, yes I try to when
Away off your place, my things and
With small eyes you peek over the edge
Making me scoff my glances sudden

Delicate to feel or even show it is
Needs to be passed then everything
Prideful eyes through which search
In me, whether I do or not, repeatedly

A simple way there could be I wish
To keep awkward moments of mess
& lastly find you reaching me fondly
To muddle my life again, again & again

15.   Dog's query

Corner he sits in, sad of heart
Eyes with cornered worry cried
Waiting poor in his own despair
Left he is alone such sometimes
& hated it is her absence much
Couldn't be done more now at
Sleep is the only abode he seeks
Then faint footsteps heard some
Raised are his brows already
Name when his called with voice
Which so held firm in his mind
Tail starts moving like a viper
Then the moment comes awaited
Forgotten all just to lick her face
Jumps the handsome with might

16.   Don't walk away

Don't walk away
It's just my life no more
Tatters my heart
Seeing you go away

Don't walk away
Can not I, laugh
Feeling yours not coming
Beside me for ever again

Poems mine have dried
Your touch is gone
Just wait is to be with you
Don't walk away

Lonely are the thoughts
You are not here
To interrupt them with
Others than yours

I cannot walk
When you walk away
Feeling nothing more
Than it's that, all is gone

"Please", can I say?
One more time
For your presence
Don't walk

17. Sometimes

Sometimes I, cry
For no special reason
Looking into loneliness
You left with me

Sometimes I, care
For no special reason
Has been only for
Me not caring anything

Sometimes I, paint
The sad colors of life
Just to feel pain at least
Blunt are the reasons of life

Sometimes I, love
To see you in everyone
Everywhere my eyes go
Substitution can not occur

Sometimes I, ignore
The facts related to you
Just to forget all that
That killed all between us

Sometimes I, need
The feeling desperately
Of you being with me
To not leave me again ever

Sometimes I forget myself
To fail to remember,
Your loss, forever
Your love subsisting severe

18. Yearning

Yearning I have of any reason,
To speak to you, anew of all
It's a wispish desire of mine,
Yet enough to conquer the realm
Of dreams of sleep every night
I see you smiling with glee
Walking together with me
Through the cranny of brown trees,
And the yellow sunshine over us
With around sweet scent of freshness
Insist I you, to walk more
Just for my earnestness to speak
Not special of any reason
But to feel your lovely presence,
In my mess of melancholy life
And so arduously you approve it
But, "wake up!" says the awakened,
Just to prove the grave invalidness
Of me, even in the dream
And in the profound yearning of you

19. Blame

I defined the distance
I created within us
Just to blame myself
As later, this day came

Some days are hard to-
Not to be numb around
When the memories come
As they are bound to come

Why is that,
Today, I love you also!
Like when, you shared
That same for me also

Selfishly I yearn more
Of your one last sight
Just to say myself then
"This won't occur again…"

I hope to see again
A beautiful time coming
When then I will dream
You talking to me again

The heart & its agony
Life dies on it
Life survives on it
Only you being my reason in it

20. Park

One time, on some day it is
A lovely occasion of you and me
On a wooden bench of a park
Resting is your head in my lap
And my fingers in your hair
Curling at their own pace
Like soothing a little child of mine
And of me rest, is book absorbed
Slightly your fingers touch my hand
Emerges my face slowly off the book,
To see a smile from corner of lips
Coyly I try to hide in my small refuge
But eyes still racing towards you
From the other side of the book
You toil to bring the sheep out again
Surrender is not given by the sheep rebel
Twitchily you turn away to gaze trees
Feeling the impatient condition of time
I start again the process of curling hair
My fingers are opposed by an angry mind
Firm persistence brings smile to your face
Following mine behind the harboring book
Happy faces turn towards each other
Hand, mine is replaced from hair to hand
And held firmly with closing of your eyes
Revisiting the book I avoid being distracted
By the book, in my thoughts of dearest you

21. Everyday

Hateful is the basketful sunshine
Seen you when, felt everyday
Temptation how much it can be?
For resisting not, the love sensation
Unbelievable hard to say you go away
When not close enough you are
Peace, how that can be achieved?
When no way to unlove someone
I find childish ways of ignoring
Resulting in pulling me deeper ever
In the dessert of delusional water
Oh dear god! Is it the only way?
Chosen to make me learn
The value of red affection
Hard to feel the blooming flower
Harder much then not to

22. Passing me

Thoughts destroy my very action
And unrest my eyes have to see
You on that turn going to home
Under my nose unaware of thus

Time is bribed, stalled & beaten
Brutally to follow but one rule
For a glance to the face divine
Passing in a second before me

Could I control my lameness?
But can't at that, sure to say
World to be stopped just for
Me to see and emotions free

Compete I my mind ugly now
Not to see, not to gaze single
Secret be risked out to you so
Ruined be my pleasured peak

23.   You

A moment of despair
A moment of happiness
Together I take with you
Life's destiny willing

Look at the flowers
And birds singing,
Living the purpose
As we ought to ours

Glimmer in dew drops
Is like shinning glory
In your eyes, I feel
When you are away

& when you are with me
Not one reason I find
To love you ever less
For eyes yours seek god

How the future awaits
I do not intend to know
Only the truth I feel
To serve almighty as one

24. Dance in the rain

To the sky when my eyes close
Rain drops fall to touch gently
Swirling on the grass a joy then
I take in one full of fresh breeze
Running from the watery rain
Under the traitor tree you watch
Just to believe what's happening
Sudden realization stops my feet
To look with blaze at you dry
Oh! You look in dilemma though
Of wish, what more beautiful to do?
To join for the rain ball with me
Or gazing mission yours of mine
Done complete under the tree
Then I threaten my dilemma to you
To drag you till wet becomes eternity
Or to splash anyway sooner or later
You laugh at my serious prospect
Heatedly back turned to you I go
A sudden hand rushes to shoulder
Making me turn around to you wet
Smiling I ruffle your wet hair
But you take my hand for the dance
Rain falls for dance's eternity
Simple rain for simple human beings
I think comes once in a while
Just for blissful ball of you and me

25. Beautiful evening

Evening was such a delight that day,
When all, for the first time, I saw in you,
That eve, flowers were so intimate,
As they came from you beautifully to me,
I remember the colorful sky turning deep
Only for me and you, wonderfully watching
Wasn't I dazed seeing the falling sun?
And only to see after, you dazed at me!
The feeling came then, wanted I to last forever
And earnestly you promised there and then
Taking my hands together confidently ever
To seek me everywhere in your world
Such wonderful, my life turned out to be
When I became only and only yours!
Couldn't I, stop crying the very moment
Calmed only by your hug to be ever together

Part II: Philosophy & Love

1. Sympathy

Could it be wrong to follow sympathy?
Strong so much to stop the world
Full of pain emotional, fatal or not
Could it be wrong to follow sympathy?
Dear ones are right, for we obstruct them
But the dearest is the culprit wanted
Could it just be the end of all good?
Death is wished in simultaneous seconds
And living consolations warns its guarantee
Is it possible or just a wholesome jinx
Feeling for disinterest arrives for beauty
And craving too arrives for rotten flesh
A flesh so real but too sour to taste
Real the beauty too of nature's own
Surrounding into its surreal paint
Question wrong of victim, to itself it is
Be gone away you sympathy wrong or not
Bliss be called my head says, scarring heart
Resurrect the butterfly be and fly away

2.   A girl described

To describe a girl magnificent
Afraid I do so to weirdest degree
Let the judges judge that be
Freedom is mine to seek feeling

And to the world what beauty is?
A lie let not be opened by mouth
Perverse are the sentences warm
Hoping to be divine but can not

Heart is raw control over issues
Of showing affection not be seen
She has the ugliness of the truth
And with features belle severe

Has then she a walk of defiance
Rioting every well gilded thought
To cherish in her boring simplicity
Her prized frame has divine fame

Sandal when embraces her feet
Smooth skin and inviting are they
Now the world sees it unappealing
Not my fault they miss Persephone

On the way I take rest to think
And mirror in, she grasps my image
For a second it is, felt communion
Eyes not but feel she seeing me

Now to her closer parts really
Lips are to be envied or desired
As a girl or lover would miss point
That they bloom in shadiest pink

Hold the thought when it explodes
Rays of attraction fatal comes
With question of reality on her side
A denied world she accepts resting

Sun you try to put behind shades
And event to seek self-denials hers
A drug making you absolute desperate
Wanting her stubborn frame clasped

Strong will hers tangled with yours
Not to envy the purpose as it be frank
But to say "mine is same, together"
Few left of us on this planet of scenic

Will then she listen to my bare plea?
Not me sir wants to deprive respect
Her need peculiar this to be satisfied
My intellect and sensitivity runs free

Let me touch her streaked fair skin
Not sympathy to console glum it is
But to kindle independence carefree
Tracing her finger tips for dance it is

Let me caresses her lips with mine
For love dwells in me of natural kind
Not versus the world nor granting it
Any part in mine, hers or whole life

Let me seek her in my castle of glee
Not a part which denies the god
With his desert of the real world
And my hand' clay at meek work

So it may put down as untold story
As for me and her sacredness only
Like it is despised to be ugly of all
Her be the best description to me

3. Delusional dream

Oh my delusional dream
What purpose you have?
To attend my mind repeatedly
Hard is to control stability
Do not you see that coming?
Or is it you need to lead me?
Somewhere not real,
A possible place of heart deep,
A world of emotional doors,
You can to & fro with desire
To imagine blissful time ahead
Delusional world becomes so real
Just when the time speaks love
Then, mine and 'his' together
There... locks cannot exist
It is so much to explore
& that so much, sometimes not
The 'him' when is not with me
Is it separation of my thoughts?
That I shouldn't take my own side
To dare to dream about him
Dream drags then further
Soul mine to bottomless pit
Of the pleasurably taken agony
Oh thy, delusional dream
Let you take my plea advice
Of coming yet again ever to me
Don't be caught by my memory
Or slaved would be us, me of you
And you of the cheerless mind

4. How to survive...

Heartbroken if you are my dear
Remind always yourself of the scar
That on your heart significant very
Tells which of the fight hardest of all
Fought for the love's little trinket

Though the same blissful itch never came
Other side from, pretence just it was
Out fronted you have honesty strong yours
So scare not now for not you are demon
To demand love, entitled for fair reason

Burn it will, like flesh cooked from inside
Try when you'll to not to hate yourself
For lowering self for love to downfall
But what better is than this making
Polishing armour of your soul to silver

Rotten, stale was the era of tolerance
May you feel to rip yourself apart
But beautiful weren't you always?
In sight of god, parents and yourself
To signify superficial partner wishes vile

Believe me now, humans need love
Very much so not to be hated again
But first of self, nurturing soul ours
Picking pieces which are cluttered
Just to make better combination of self

Compete not yourself then for revenge
By finding another one in front of eyes
Spirit of strongest kind resides in you
To fool yourself for another passion
Worldly it is, lowly for the true inside

Evil mind tempt you not its fastidiousness
Be patient for the cause worth living a life
Survive to try again & again true love
Truly it always stays whether you fail or win
When you listen to it and not mind

And finally when you let go of it all
Learn to get hold again of the chances
Not to obtain love of fill the space
But to share the love honest of kind
For the tale to spring like flower again

5.   A rose in my yard

There I saw her wrapped up
Green blankets warm as wool
Red is your talent as it can be
My yard waited a long to have
Striker beautiful to stand alone
A rose not yet fulfilled its days
But to say I couldn't sorry you
World is far to cruel to exist

Troubles come soon to you
When you bloom to be young
A way can't I find of abiding
Morbid is it for you my dear?
Imagine me watching you fade
Wishing why we destined meet
Just to find a moment to feel
Nothing more than petty love

6. White paper gifts

White papered gifts, you mean-
A way to give thoughts
Something bland in manner
But see the white serenity again
Calmest expressions are they!
Without anything of confusion
A superior love of human being
Just conveyed so simply

What will you ever think?
It is when a token to you
Of my feeling unarticulated
But they are the only one
Natural so much it can be
All colors reflecting in one
Like love of many moods
Only for one true person

Gifts covered in this blank
Just tells a different story
Where bliss is considered
For someone, heartily giving
And happiness conceived
For someone, heartily taking
And true the story becomes
When exchange such seen

Something I mean to give you
Someday, just like this, in white
With little bit of ardour laid
And with little bit of argument
Oh! Just don't say thank you!
Shy I become at such then
Like that white paper gift
Can't I, say anymore then!

7.   A sad storm

A storm comes by and by
To every emotional sea unawake
Deep pierced are the elements
For incense, till death of them

I turn away to every morsel
Aliveness of which seeks in me
For dead are the thin veins
Dead is the intellect

What conditions to be put?
For the simple life broken
Regaining its peaceful ordinance
Just to be found in someone

Valor my valor where it is!
Every day the search begins
I wait to see it found
Wait to be gained in me

Sad are never the feelings
Yet valor is sought desperately
For sad imports are feared
Of not faceable personification

Misery still loved dearly
Of parting with torn soul
Then filthy fast emotions
Of living mouthful lie as truth

It is not the love, weakens
But profoundness of feelings seen
As loving is able contently
With no tint of flawed mortality

Happy are the words and laws
Such when storm replied by me
In midst of emotional gashing
A satisfaction is, loving truly

8. Decisions

Decisions I thought then
Could never go wrong
For regret to grasp my mind
About the social life of unsocial

It ought to happen
Still it comes to my mind
But could love sacrificed behind?
To look back off the shoulder

Rude can be the life often
If you give her sour grapes
After all, give & take process she is
You get what you adoringly give

It is not about differences you seek
Or alikeness to talk love
It is just the reason to part away
Not understanding the attachment

Gems are the funny objects
The stones which shine
Humans alike shine differently
Just to find, which to you shine

Have you never fallen in love?
That's what loners ask
They do not have love
Could that to be found

9. Or

To be or not to be...
If that's the question,
It serves no answer to me
I can not be that one ever
You desire for yourself
But I really know about me
That inexpressible love I have
To be or not be loved by you
That desire always, to be with you
Even may you not speak a word...
That will, to see you happy,
To be or not to be, I the reason for
That freedom, to adore you
Even may it, not clue you ever
I, to be or not be?
If that's the question of matter,
It serves no matter anymore

10. Game of love

A game of secret love
That's what we play
Everyday is new chance
To prove love unsuspicious

Imagination is to be hard
For the muddle we get in
In situation such as this
Trying all is mandatory

Is it art or science?
Or plus, minus or normative?
To be in eyes of one, seen to
All's 'shall be ignorant eyes'

Hard to know game reality
Or is it coincidental illusion
Harder to cure such ever,
Say or not to say which is

Still though the pleasure
Assuming of returning love
One unwilling to quit, unless
Miracle takes you someway

It is a strange awful risk
Something of heart is lost
Whether the lottery ticket
Won or lost at the end

11.   Weirdness

Weird having it is
Pain to be beautiful
No love investment
Business mind it is

When you have all
Running for stinks
Of unrelated goals
Is it not uncommon?

Puzzling are leaves
Fallen red collectible
Or mindful rainy green
For beautiful to decide

Exploring little earth
Living one life alike
Facing the medium
Of sad, happy feelings

No good the three any
End, start or process
Of the soul joining
Look for fourth thing

Surety to understand
Nothing to be there
It is mind revolving
Again around me only

12.   I ask myself

I ask myself,
Is that what I was?
Not to mention the silence,
Unclear is my rational cause

I ask myself,
Was there no mercy?
Which should, I have asked!
For sole betterment of me

I ask myself,
Why is such a self denial?
Don't I need myself?
To give the penance reliable

I ask myself,
Is that why you went away?
To set down this world alone
Turning me in two ways

I ask myself,
Why are feelings so numb?
Have I forgot to miss you
Or painful the world has become

I ask myself,
To ask you of such way
Which goes off from me,
Turning again in my way

I ask myself,
Is there any question
Which will answer for me,
The evidence of love sensation

13. What I want?

Somber, somber are my lips!
To touch the words,
I couldn't shout...

Stopped, yes stopped are those ships
Which are yet to be gone
To their desired destiny

Numb! Have become numb, the meanings
Of my sentimental life,
Yet that to be fallen by age

Falls everything around, it falls!
When I stare you with me
Raising things again around

Delicate are feelings, very delicate!
For you, of mine,
If you ever want to accept

Day by day, it goes ever
Whatever may be the reason
To remain silent as before never

Want? What is that I want?
For I and you- us together
Or me the sole traveller

14. Sailing of my life

For the sailing of my life
Azure water is a necessity
To see reflection of me and
You aside, smiling with me,
And there is a need of mighty cial
To praise the mightiness of dear god
Will go then we to the seven seas
To enlighten the poor siblings
By his knowledge & our kind ability
Adventure beautiful, isn't this really?
For the service devoting completely
All I ask to myself, to be ready
& you to accompany me, marching
Hand in hand, till our end should be!

15. Blank page

A blank page stares at me
Blankly the intentions conveyed
Colorful twists aren't with him
Imaginations mine are to be, they!

There is something more such
My life, frankly very blank
Here though the twists not usual
They are indirectly wanted

Much it is to crave blank page
Mortal wants usual, usually
It wants you to be with me
Normally our life to begin

Colors imagined say differently
Distance is the final twist
Challenging the every minute
To get even psyched with you

Oh! Page and my wilful colors
Fictions created for only reason
Distant pieces of you in me
Filling heart always & together

16.   Agony or guilt

Preference to the question
Of agony or guilt, selected
Which shall be so quickly?
To get you fair & square

It is a wilful chance taken
Of the not wilful desires
What does it matters, again?
I lose every time whatever may

How can you stay quiet?
When you ought to be true
Possessively taking me
From my only possession

Dreams often come of you
Possible of right way ahead
I do not understand now
Which side should I take?

There are so many fences
Couldn't you break them?
Forbidden me lay inside
In your arms for resting

A buzz of muddle water
Is world, where untangles
The soul mate you for me
But for me not to reap

17. Silly emotions

Stupendous emotions
Of unending love
Bugs throughout a day
Sting of bees alike

No one can see
Burning sun at day
Mind of money used
True heart of behaving

In a corner, I lay down
Stripes of light, evening
Gaze my silent picture
Stating my psyche alive

Styles of color of love
Makes all spiritual
Nothing much of existence
It's all given up

Next are strokes of light
No white, only purity
Of my life for love
Are the silly emotions

18.   Shiny bond

Can I confirm myself?
It's not obsession
Nor it is love
Something more than love

It's just the voice I hear,
Tingles me, not to touch you
But just to feel the soul
Same as mine, in you

More than love, I find
What's that in the world?
Nothingness of me and else,
Everything to you surrendered

Love is just mere bond
Shines every first time
When I see you
Banking more for next time

Lucky am I to be afraid
To think of losing you
When we say our goodbye
Wish is granted every time

Separation I do not fear
It is the awful dust, to us
Comes, of forgetfulness
When under it bond disappears

When comes the end
And when it begun
We may know, or not
But bond, united we know

19. Zeal

Oh the hideous zeal,
Of blameful ruler of mind
Hurt thy innocent life
Deep colors run down white

User of the inspection glass
Eyes our tangled relation
To find pleasure in agony
Of ourselves from each other

Whistled was the plain air
With sweet music of love
So it is now with love only
True to itself more than ever

Hurt whenever I am
Name I only yours drive
To remind consciously myself
Solace of complete life

Reading through the sighs
There is a world beyond my eyes
In dreams that I can find
Comes in waiting for you

Enough for me it is
When I see you feel for me
But decide never to reply when
A new relation ours begins

20. Question

If you are not cheerful
You ought to be sad
Easy is not, my-
Every day and night

If you can't tell me
I ought not to know it
That's what is all
Want I, to know about

If you still so love me
Why ought to separate?
When future is known
Ourselves we change

If you want me unaltered
Why accept me not even!
Confusion it is just to be
To be what around you?

If you never recall me
Why of all, I am evoked?
Such turmoil it is just,
Once, to think of you

If love I have yet much
Why can't I be with you?
Erasing your every sorrow
Instead being in sorrow

If that's how path goes
It is ought to be followed
What is ought to happen
Let then it be happened

21.　Prologue

Words are sought empty to begin
Hollow is deep down the expression
When thoughts decide to come
Of opaque destiny to you

And there is no return when
Given the thought away finally
I sadly amaze at my wonder
That have ever yet not it given

Purpose is what then again
Of the words so ardently written
They are just the blunt thorns
Not hurtful but sensed as gone pain

Fear is not with me anymore
Nor the attitude of the lost one
Hope is though always true friend
No matter how the darkness surrounds

With no grace I see the people
Never there is a pity to store
A plea though not to find weakness
In myself when I see you again

Though missed are those days
Painted in radiant colors of earth
Love was that way described mine
But as water you flowed away

22. Sounds

Sounds of turning edge
Sharp the pains of mind
Listen to the water drop
Patience violent it tells
Not to stand shallow
For the meaning of life
Broken hearted died
A long ago the memories
Knowing to be independent
Dependent I became
Against to it, prove myself
People get hurt, don't they?
Cannot simply tell I to them
What a statue sensitive I am!
Cry to the sad piano piece
When I have lost you, I do
But love I don't to you
It's that the only confusion
Face I everyday through

23. Invitation

Why should you be heard now?
Complication has reached to most
Of relation understood not at all
Then with what seeks the severity

Pushed was I & when I was pushed
Rushed my feelings with poison red
To seek just not you in my mind
Desperate to live, pursuing wounds

And when I grasped tryingly the last
Effervescence yours left with soul
Eroded slowly Iron of my strong will
To the pit of deepest want & dark

Though you are going far so away
You need what kind of pleasure?
Seeking my sympathy in process
Thinking I would give in so easily

Although now soft side kicks word
Describe to what was hidden a long
Scared by the failure, rejection more
And to the most simplest 'no' fatal

Nights when I could not sleep least
Reason had not been heartache
But the necessity to feel even blue
Been gone much to be just numb

And instant then you want moment
Again scratching what is to be lost
Derivation tries to pursue me deep
To find longer pit to be discovered

Scorn is it or happiness reflection its
Mind my grasps firmly holding at that
Smiles don't indulge my face these days
But do when I, believe it to be wicked

There is even somebody else now
To care wisely of emotions flowing
In a way which be termed so happy
Why should you be heard now?

24. Rain

Rain is like emotional weep
Pouring out of my heart
Clouded by distances of worlds
Waiting for sunshine of life,
Forms the bond which
Of god to mortal sound
Like me unbound
To shine in a rainbow royal

I crave for that sunshine
For that god of mine
Take as offering, a loving heart
Take me as a part
Part of the rainbow
& I'll never miss a song
For the sunshine it rains
And shines the sun for the rains

25. Distance

Distance is the question
Never to be solved for me
Should the sun not rise?
For the rule of the mortal king
Should not I come near you?
For non existing conflicts
Should the knowledge stop?
For ignorance to change its side
Should I not ever love you?
Cause you hate this liking of me
Closeness of you is a lie
And distance is the question...

Part III: Philosophy

1. Tell me your fear

Then you must have a fear
What if you see a lire ghost?
Lurking for your sight near by
Grabbing you in a corner thick
Then you must have a fear
No? Then what if the monster
Green in shade puke grinning
Slimy hands with skin burns
Then you must have a fear
Things we see not in dailies

What if jackal comes running?
Slimy, his teeth with your sight
Eyes fiercely fixed on flesh hot
Excited by the pray weakling
Then you must have a fear
No? Still then what of venom?
Creeping on to your nerves
Snake fanged black bit you in
Circled and dancing over head
Things we do so see day's sight

Then you must have a fear
What if mutilator enjoys ride
With you, tearing live pieces
Agonizing is your head to toe
Till death might be only wish
No? What if body is beautiful?
Seen yours as the utility filing
To force the rubbing avarice
Making the pride scream mercy
Things human do to each other

Then you must have a fear
What if thief is strong to steal?
The ring, lover passionately gave
Off your finger off your heart
Not even at the moment's time
No or may be just the lover ran?
Far from you, without a reason
To tell your aching heart it's ok
Fearing all other would be same
Things are thus we consider life

What if the leaders you follow,
Seek revenge on your honesty
Greed of your happiness calm
Turning societies against you
Then you must have a fear
But not, what if you one stand
Against the wrong to right it
But knowing it's not tradition
All of them despise true of you
Things we call conceit that is

What if they burn you on steak?
For seeing the god as it wants
And to follow the law of martyr
Caring not the word of priest
Who abode in the temples high,
Then you must have a fear
To destroy the existence real
For people want it to be as them
Fake as they can show more each
Things they decide instead god

Then I must not at all have fear
Reason for it to be my integrity
God to be the faith confided in
Flesh may torn apart at heart
They can't touch the soul a bit
Let them deal the green devil
Inside theirs so fighting himself
Manipulating the hardened lives
Fear even comes be overawed
Then I must not at all have fear

2. Attention

Attention! Attention!
Here comes the sun
To brighten your ways
And minds to the further
People-why do you go around?
Don't you need a bag?
Full of light to pass around
I agree, there is no brand tag
But do you need that
When all marts are in his sack
Little by little and more by more
That's the way we learn
The knowledge of god's world
And so the tutor has come,
To enlighten our mortal world
Why, shouldn't we pray now!
For the healthy mind
Directed towards god's holy sign!

3.   Picture

Picture stolen of the mind gallery
Leaves behind evidence of time
Guilty against passing itself
What's the use of lamenting?
If the picture isn't returning
Or no actions to be taken, it for
What nonsense to miss me!
If to me no regards are to talk
A widow cries on a river
For her existence or his death!
Confused is the poem at goal
And me to express the moment
Call it good or bad, I judge not
For understanding my soul
To where, its rapid going
If tomorrow picture retrieved
Or tried to be gained by you
There is question of distance
Whether to awake me by time

4. Awaken

My eyes when close in a moment
What if I wake up dream from this!
Would all be same? Of known earth
They say not death but else it is,
To realize reality in a flies' wing flap
Closing of lids on eyes and opening
Divinity for to behold of truth it is
Care pulls behind and always near
Herself to her arms for all the love
Gone is a divine, eye when opens

5. Secret desire

Looking at the eclipses of land
By walking steady feet of mine
Shows the way of unending search
God, you come on finder's path
Divider's wealth I do not seek
Fortune real is specialist's specialty
Reserved fangs of the mortal life,
So beautiful they always seem to be
Poisonous with ignorance though
Held tight by us to ourselves,
Gives us boon or curse of 'to desire'
Wish to destroy wishes leads to god
& that wish also not wished by god
Cultures and their so many countries
Seeing them on my way somewhere
Ascetic I walk in this urban world
As a being involved in earthly love
Keeping a secret desire to me
To go far away from all the love
To find it again at the same destiny

6. Bridge of the waterfall

Reflections when dive in deep blue
Primitive catches the particle small
Of soul through we live at time sun
And through the moon we dream
Night and the world are left then
To their fate to show truth desired
Remembrance is prohibited to seek
Know we not the source of being

Places sought are actualized directly
Consciousness itmay or not relate
One of my friends in particles drags
The whole dough to an ocean deep
Thrown are the human beings alike
Verve mine in water numb to feel
Objective to not really cruel of them
To swim where I could find approval

Others there are without identity of
And the snakes of fat bodies flow
How humorous that we cross roads!
Afraid both we are of our niche' end
Though there are some dead on top
Snakes with white tabs & green & men
Query is to avoid how the touch theirs
Continued, like the apocalypse none

But I touch a little to wiggle one alive
Dead he was thought flowing by side

With certainty was it accident or will
Mind is already scared to realize this
Does not he open mouth to bite but
Swims by me like a rope swift in line
Skin mine gave him vivacity is it true?
Or tinged was my spine at tip's end?

It has been so against the flow I will
Back I swim to find land with river
And piece of stone sought at when
Cling to is the wish the bridge above
Shagged and rotten wood its skeleton
Shelled but such as the longest corridor
Brown paper crumpled such are walls
Legs through which gushes azure mass

Fog though covers when I search land
Both sides such have extent to infinity
Abode ascended to seek cover of rain
Corridor long wooded, of walls brown
Shakes wind to the hideous condition
But I know though inside, water falls
Sound of the huge pouring touch ears
Beautiful blue mass attracts me more

Now when recognition each possible
Family are they I see, all at together
Close is my cousin with me to seek
But to fall edge on the corridor gallery
Saves my mind, there is hard flooring
Others intend to dine, set quickly at
But not hear our plea to keep going
To find the extreme any or the exit

Sit when we to dine lost at debate
Thoughts tangle how long to crash
Temporary the abode we refuge in
Fear strikes of existence unreal be
Left are others every one of them
And I run long to the similar way
With no trace of land to the bridge
End' what then I question myself

Diving back to river would solve it?
Existence illusionary, consumes me
Or falling off the waterfall roaring
Kill the hand of faux over my skin
Can't be out if, I should behave ill
But stops the good angel conscious
There is way, as something I know
Loved by me of the realest world

Remember when I the being loved
Will destroys its imitation of fake
Patches surround me now coloured
Bodies fly to none, sounds to mum
Sight is cleared and eyes opened
One existence just died to one alive
Though arms I see around love mine
Reality is a question of other time

7. Wait

"Wait! Oh wait!" says the time,
"A moment comes here for you
Brings a colorful face to your sketch
A song of love for your calmness
Flowers scented with fresh water breezes
And lastly with a touch of 'care'
No chance for you to desire anymore!
Only condition I put together to it...
Moment has to pass away for the next"
Without a breathe I say, "I accept"
So I wait and wait...
When it does come once in a while
To me, carrying you along the tide
My heart cannot be ever satisfied
I try to bribe the time
All other moments for that one...
Nothing does that of, works
But still I do wait
Wait for over again...

8.   World to a loser

World to a loser
A venomous snake
Coiling around him
To push him around

World to a loser
A dangerous art
Made of lucky things
To be failed in total

World to a loser
Is a fight for happiness
With unfair measures
Always taken smaller

World to a loser
Is a complex mystery
Desiring moral only
Immoral have him only

World to a loser
Is as just losing one
Love truly loved
A trifle amount for reason

World to a loser
Dumb to understand
Deep feelings of mind
Just gone on shell things

A loser to world
Is only a loser
Left to himself alone
Used by owns way

9.   Insecurity

How it feels to be drastically fallen?
Out of eyes, out of the own respect
Smash you need to everything else
Everything you find related to self

May it rain, and to be wished rain
There is need of bravery enough
To bring down every point of hill
Courage but have gone to ashes

Compile when you the honour left
Defeat of which you desire cling
Ego rebels of your meagre being
To just present a show unfruitful

Prepared be reader for I sure tell
Truth about the human adversity
And it is the bitterest kind to see
That real is nothing that is glorious

To seek the pleasure in little things
Can be your best mistake of life
And even when you try, you will
Find it enticing to break off then

Hardly should you try to hear all
The bit a sound of the footsteps
Can't, won't you succeed never
Star had already fallen of the peak

Then what is praise and who to like
Lonely vigor should be sought now
Nothing could cure the mistrust so
Spoiled is the angel had been ours

To stay away is the biggest agony
Bet you could scratch yourself with
Sufferance is your drug to endure
Or live in the well of rabid thoughts

Trace of real breaks my pretence
Expectation proved in will's favour
Love returns to the love given by
Traced are the eyes forgetting rift

Such foolishness seems the phase
Spent it in an utter anger conceit
Fulfilled now with very existence
Heart can ever want nearest to be

10. Alive Mirror

Why so painful to be alive to be a mirror?
Truth is all that I have to show
And really do I work it lively
That, others think I am like them
As they are...for only themselves
But only until you come to see deep in me
When I become one image of you
I feel my heart with you
But, ...wonder how should I describe you?
A mirror in dilemma...?
Can't show your beautiful heart,
For me as simple mirror just
And as a being alive I am
Necessity it is to show you all felt
So painful to be alive therefore
But though more, inanimate if, to not feel you

11.   Existence

A light said to another in hurry
You are me, silly also to say this
Reply was weirder more of mate
Do not I exist without beholder?

Warns then listening this beholder
Shut be the chitchat or my eyes close
When a voice intersect the threat
Oh fool! Close them & be enlightened

And enlightened then implored self
Do you exist? Do you exist ever sir?
Answer didn't seem to roam around
When alien help lighted on other fact

Quiet not changing confidence, it layed
Darkness that, who had the final word
It crept in slowly its hand in front
Hissing, "thus that's why you exist!"

12. Hail the leader

Hail the literate leader
One of a kind he is
Among the lusty mongrels
Shouting a meaningful word

Hail the murderous leader
Simply which he did
Of the awful creeping
In people's mind of sin

Hail the dictator commander
For he is the ruler extreme
Of one rule, god & race
& the scam of bad ego scares

Hail the fasting gentleman
Who eats not on behalf of
Known or unknown name
The gold or silver of poor

Hail leader's good and bad,
Who fought for your good
Because for bad in him
There is another in waiting

13. A day

A day yet has to show us
When tragedy will be merry
I talk about the mere truth
It will concern us later
Thinking about the tragedy
The biggest is to be death
On a mortal's mind
Shouldn't I think of the one?
Where is the pious mind?

A day yet has to show us
When realization will be done
Of distinguishing the facts
To real and mortal beings
But clear the things become
Only when end commence
I earnestly call to you all
For there may be a second yet
To honour the almighty, first!

14. An outsider jaw

Thought my brain was falling out
To the deft I can't yet see, once
But resisted the mind for logic
And gave permission otherwise
To take out the jaw with all teeth
Pretend when I to clean them
Realized is, how clean words are
As I speak all fine through them
Unable to fix though the tragedy
Mute I walk in hand white teeth
They see the horror and grasp
Can't be explained but not it is so
Truth they didn't want of mouth
Which mine intended to speak,
Thus fleshed jaw resting outside
And roams me unable to lie even
Seeking doctor of divine integrity
Somehow to channel the rebel in

15.   Song & the storyteller

It all started one day
When I found myself
Around a intimate song
Sung beautifully for me

Here were those trees
With grave expressions
Of those poignant music
Like a French horn alone

With the company of viola
Just came by then, calmly
As the tranquil river flowed
Gray in its own way near by

Just had to be spicy now
Bird's twitter I heard
Like hundred piccolo eager
Talking to each other

Joined in the clarinet solo
Without any request asked
By a lone little white goat
Lost in heeding birds

Then drums had to be there
By the thumps of a herd
Grazing with bells neck tied
As another background music

A feeling touched heart,
Like, hands touching sky lean
There was a smooth wind
With I sang happy mong ming

Small such is the merriment
Conceived this when I,
Song sang its blissful story
I a part of, being storyteller

16. The grief

Oh! The grief of these people
Is without hope and peace
All is the need of moment
To satisfy the thirst of anger

Oh! The grief of these people
Creates incurable grief for others
To prove themselves is the cause,
Why innocent people should die?

Oh! The grief of these people
For the god's favourable wish
Or for own intimate desire
To say- satisfy we, god from us

Oh! The grief of these people
Is not amendable for the reason
Of their ignorable hardened hearts
They run away from themselves

Oh! The grief of these people
Testify the moral ones though
They are learnt to forgive
Seeing the greater grief of others

Oh! The grief of these people
Makes grave people yet more
To forget happy and faithful world
& to only deliver misery over all

17.   The light & its wisdom

Sun setting its luxuriance
As to take away memory
Of the unworthy takers
Believing in little lamps

Small illumination of them
To show the setting sun
Of the evening civilization
A happy thing for fake liking

Wisdom is the easy word
For advice and saying others
Wisdom meant by heart
Is known by seekers

Seekers seek the sun in dark
Knowing it only real exists
For the betterment of others
Keeping own desires aside

Takes care of them the sun
As the sun again rises
For they are the care takers
With no care for themselves

No theory or law for figuring
Just a supreme freewill
Thus sun is not for solving
To be but knowing & feeling

Sun sets for the opportunity
To began to have your wish
Not for the need of wish
Desire which people of night

18. Raindrops

They fall, they fall
Like clustered souls
Wind of pre-rain
Is just so beautiful

Dry seeds of those
Green trees in ascesis
Fall, they fall, they fall
Just to be wet in coming rain

Fragrance of the land
Joy it is, of the heart
To feel it to yourself, and
Know not what to do with it

A simple mind for it is
To the sudden rain of summer
On to sacred contentment
Of life utterly beautiful

Road greased tar black
Water becomes to be living
A traveller as for me
Has to be happy being alive

Lively drops of the sky
Is such a honest gift
To the angrily dried wife
As peace begot to her children

19. Fighting souls

A tumult has taken lead
The thousand shores fight
Humanity its soul enemy
Shield and lances none on side

Refuge, Oh joyful refuge
Where might we seek?
Cowardly confidence we amuse
Humanity pretends to be weak

Acumen is rightful act of god
Needed is to be comprehended
Denies it, the man's broken side
Wants fall in ignorance's keep

At the war's end finally then
Desires of the Promised Land
When destroyed are the means
Doubtful are to be reached

Time heals the deep wounds,
Fire and vengeful behaviours
But could time be healed?
Of knots of dead within

Then could souls have future?
Among the peaceful destiny
Face of earth on which
Faithful entity when destroyed

Keep not, Oh shores of human
The ugly sea of cowardice
Humanity calls with soft voice
To shield the innocent kind

20.   Traveller

A thing to be hated most
Puzzle it is to quickly realize
Looking onto a tree waded road
No other white thought is admitted

Nor is it easy either the distance
To calculate between mind & its space
I walk around when around the sea
It imagines the space far away

Could think then for what to be gain
When all I do without purpose to sail
Love, hate or any intimate delicacy it is
More it can't be then desire's taste

Birds fly when far away from me
Indifference I cannot feel about
Beauty fills me, in abundant
With life of vigorous life seeker

There are the flowing waves
Trying to fall behind separately
For running world wants to be fast
Desire they complete of the runner

What questions be forgotten most
Life isn't so complicated yet
They aren't about fast or slow
'Running for' serves the answer

Soon it would have changed air
Waves realize & so does the sea
Service couldn't be altered though
A rule of death & life seems to be

All the faces they have seen
With the piteous fake ignorance
They express not in simple to & fro
Runners seek their own to comprehend

Then someway could I understand?
To write an obstinate poem
To seem I may have stopped because
To realize running left me by far

21. Proud heart

Sighs I try to control through
Weeping of my proud heart
Relevance is given easy & cool
Still again & again are they used!

To prove ourselves to be good
Others are just need to be used
Where are the real feelings?
To satisfy the real meanings

Qualify the label of mannerism
Shall I bow to a drunkard extreme?
Just the false notions these are!
To complete our sinister needs

Hated are those little ones
For the betterment of big people
Who divulge people to themselves!
In a way, of working shamelessly

Afraid become then these
Of losing the morbid wealth
Wonder it is, when they know
Forever, it, they will never own

Not am I a very wise person
Just that I believe though
True feelings always remain true
True meanings always gain truth

22.   Self protection

Will the shatters earn?
To willful caress mine
Windows free the cold
Of the ages with sick belief

Too much it is to be patient
Not much to kill, soul mine
Where is now the armor?
Protect, I need to, innocence

I try to be the worst ultimatum
Morality is pestering friend
Such I think always then
To console myself wrongly

Complain, I do not intend
In the world, letting in
But abuse they me why?
Reason none given from me

How easy they seem all!
To adapt uncaring practices
Self is not the only person
Hard hearted they themselves

23. Words of black ink

Words of black ink & tear drop
Feelings show as the smudge
Writer's telepathy it is
Pleased the reader's hungry soul be!

Compacted are the colors
Black & white they chose to be
Just to give the feelings are colors
Realization of words thrive on it

Letters aren't all flowery
To make anybody cry
Those are the unseen silk threads
Joining heart to heart by letters

Writer asks for a reply
But that is not often written
Some things are to be told
Some should be known by own

24. Light and shadows

These shadows hide
For the dense fear
Of losing themselves
Light enlightens true self

Shadows are the darkest dark
People to whom they belong
Hided behind, like a child
A broken mistake from parents

But what ignorance small it is!
Not realized by stupid shadows
Exist they because of light
How would hiding ever be?

Light doesn't reveal that either
Would a parent if they love?
Shadow owners need trust
To accept the enlightened ness

Shadow is important but very
To the owners life
Though the shadow dark
Light is realized through it

25. Entrapment

Behold says my head
Pain of the entrapment
A Jail emotional around

They who are called popular
Realize not the obvious bars
When the questions of freedom

Help can never be option
If need it is not of indulgence
When color false shine eyes

Oh fools are there only some
Other wash hands in river flow
Fulfilling wishes of inside void

Fear not light says does it not?
Good resides in whom need it is
And who implore its delegation

Printed in the United States
By Bookmasters